Popular Teaching Resources

Canadian Character Education

Grades **3-4**

Janet Bartier • William Young

Printed in China

Contents

Guidelines for Use

This resource book contains two sections:

- Core Units
- Project Ideas

Each **Core Unit** is made up of a lesson and follow-up worksheets. You will see that in all of the units, "Name", "Date", and the unit topic appear on each follow-up worksheet, so that each one can stand on its own. There is more than one way to present each unit in the book. Here are two that may work for you: (1) give your students the lesson and the worksheets at the same time and let them work on both simultaneously; (2) give just the lesson one day and ask your students to underline key words and ideas or take notes as you talk about the subject, and then give them a worksheet the next day as a quiz.

The **Project Ideas** give students the opportunity to do independent research and then share it with the rest of the class. You may want to adapt them to be up to date with current events.

Happy teaching!

Canadian Character Education Grades 3-4

Core Units

Name: Date:

Compassion

Mr. Baron asked his class for suggestions on how they could practise compassion.

"We could collect old winter coats and take them to the homeless shelter," said Dylan.

"Showing concern for others' warmth in the winter is compassionate," Mr. Baron agreed. "Great idea!"

Pria put up her hand. "We could send Luke a "Get Well" card. He's been away sick all week."

"Yes," said Mr. Baron. "That would be a wonderful way to show we care."

Mr. Baron and his class decided to do both right away. Some started planning the winter coat collection, while others started drawing Luke's card.

While they worked on their compassionate projects, something interesting happened. They worked happily but quietly because the class next door was having an important test. Some of the children shared their pencil crayons with Deanna, who had forgotten hers at home. And later, at lunch, two kids shared their lunch with David, who had lost his on the way to school.

Mr. Baron's class could not wait to get out of the classroom to show compassion; they realized they already practised it in their daily lives at school. They showed sympathy towards the other class's need for quiet, and easily shared with those in need of pencil crayons and lunch.

Compassion is being sensitive to what others need, and doing our best to provide what we can.

Name: Date:

Compassion

Brainstorm different ways you could practise compassion with your friends.

Practice 1

- Someone in need: ____________________
- What is needed: ____________________
- What we can provide: ____________________

____

Practice 2

- Someone in need: ____________________
- What is needed: ____________________
- What we can provide: ____________________

____

Practice 3

- Someone in need: ____________________
- What is needed: ____________________
- What we can provide: ____________________

____

Name: Date:

Compassion

Colour the puzzle pieces that contain words related to compassion.

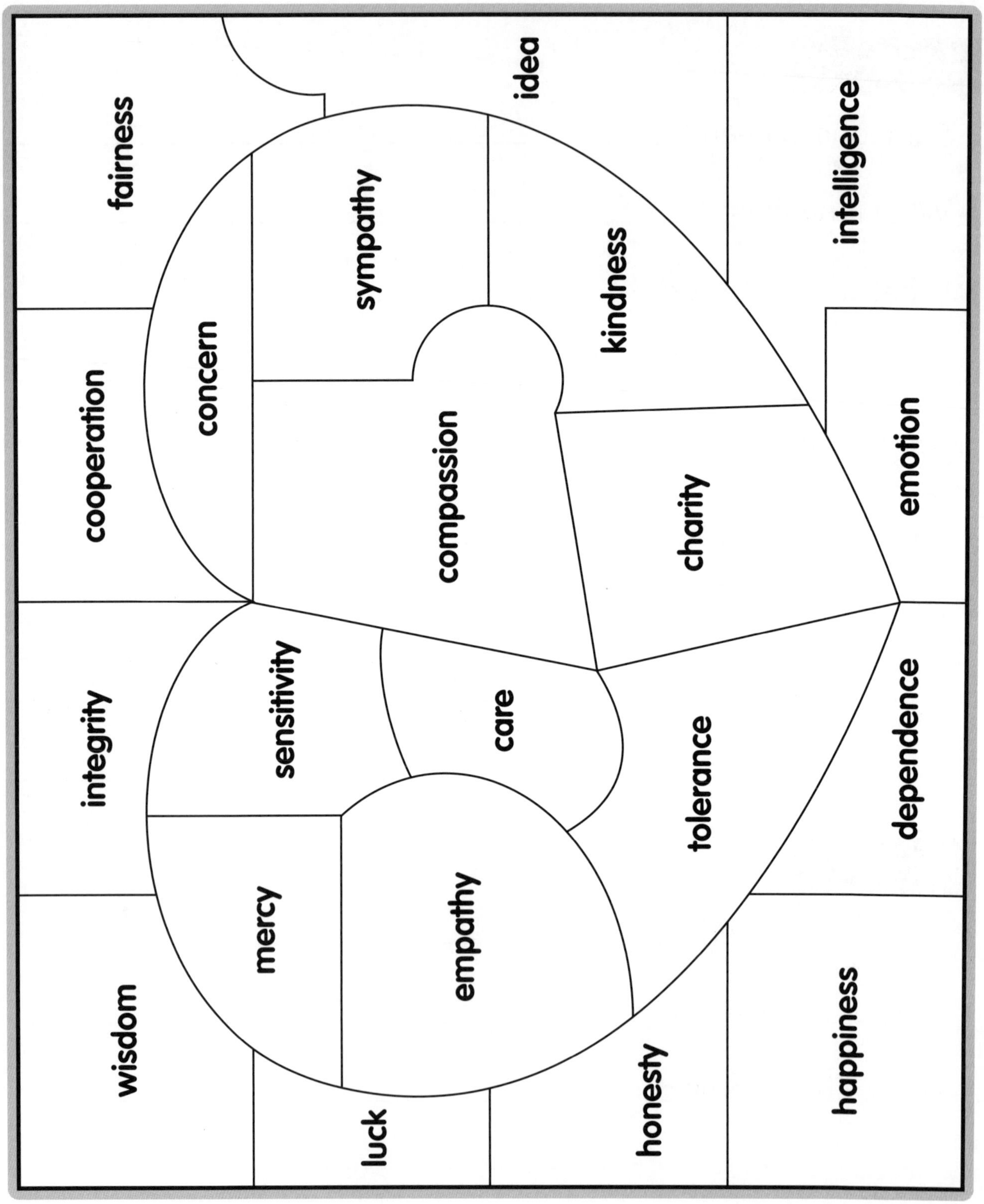

Name: Date:

Compassion

Answer the questions and complete the sentences.

1. How would you feel if other children laughed when you gave a wrong answer to the teacher?

____

When someone else gives a wrong answer to the teacher, I will ______

____

2. How would you feel if you forgot to bring a snack for school?

____

When someone forgets to bring his or her snacks for school, I will ____

____

3. 

How would you feel if you were the new kid in the class?

____

When there is a new kid in my class, I will

____

____

Name: Date:

Compassion

Make up a short slogan that will encourage others to practise compassion towards one another. Use the slogan in a T-shirt design.

care concern sympathy kind

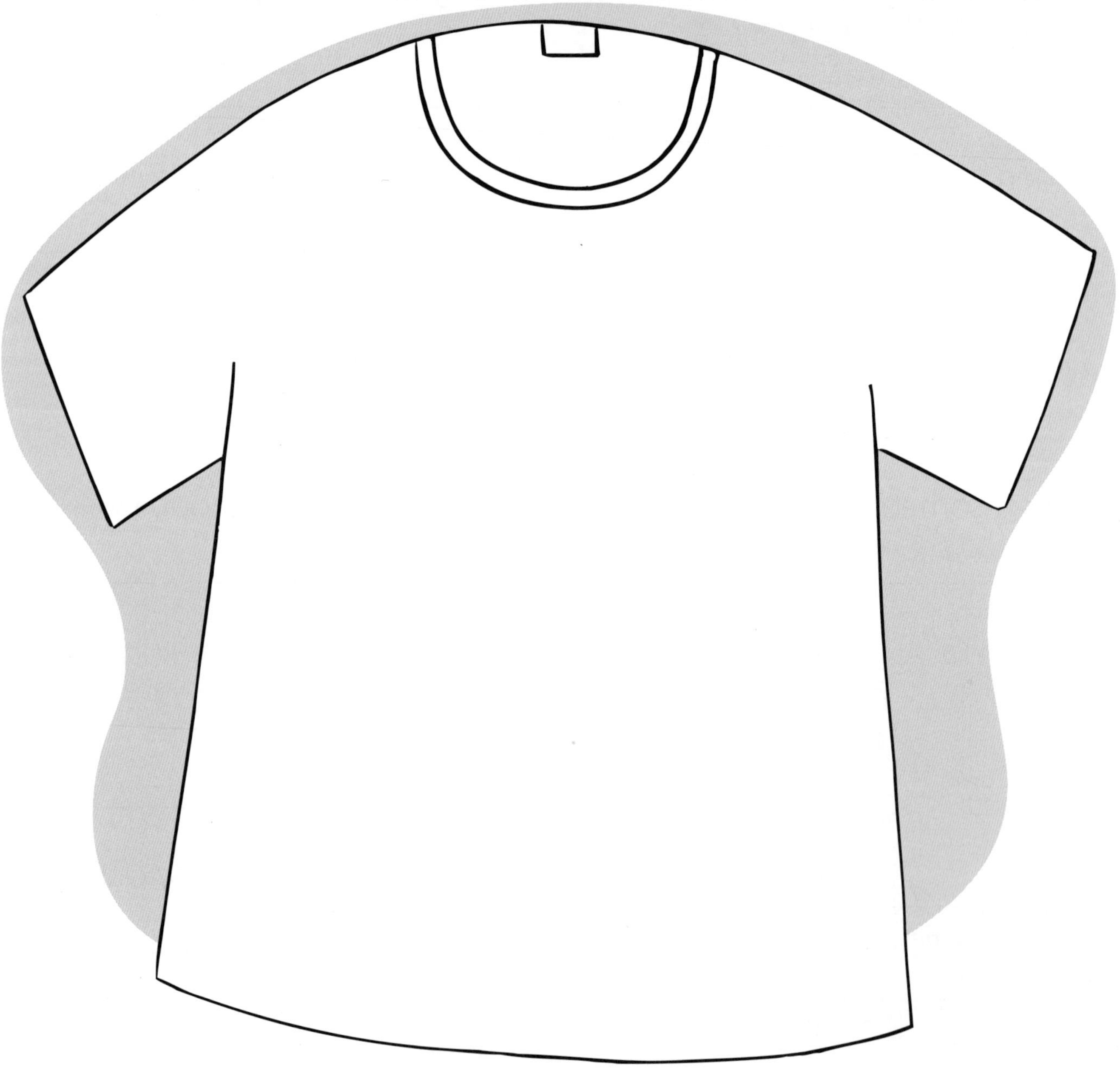

Name: Date:

Compassion

Find a story about a compassionate act from a newspaper or magazine and paste it to this page. Then share your feelings about this story. Share an event you witnessed or experienced that you felt was compassionate.

A Compassionate Act

My Experience with Compassion

Name: Date:

Honesty

Honesty can be seen in many forms. Telling the truth is honest. But being dependable to people that count on you and fair with people you deal with is honest as well.

What happens when we are not honest? Have you ever told one lie only to find you needed to tell more lies to keep from being found out on the first one? In the end, a web of lies traps only the person who spun it.

When we are honest, no matter what the consequences, we will be believed when it is most important, and considered trustworthy to others. Most importantly, we can be at peace with ourselves.

Name: Date:

Honesty

Sort the words into the correct columns.

honourable	loot	deceive	fair	reliable
corrupt	reputable	devious	rob	sincere
fraud	cheat	truthful	integrity	unfair
direct	frank	lie	cheat	dependable

Honest	**Dishonest**

Name: Date:

Honesty

Read what Derek says. Answer the questions.

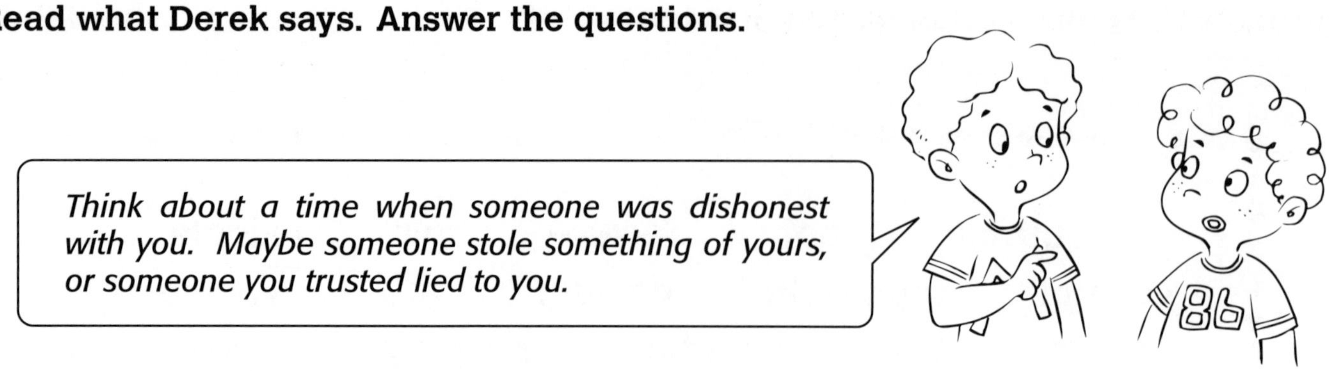

1. How do you feel when people are dishonest with you?

2. Why is it important that people are honest with you?

3. How do you feel when you are not honest with people?

4. Why is it important that you are honest with others?

Name: Date:

Honesty

For each dishonest action, write if it is best described as "untruthful", "unreliable", or "untrustworthy". Then think of what the honest reaction would be and write it on the lines.

1. You are at your friend's house, and you find a coin on the floor.

   You put it in your pocket. ← [ ]

   ______________________ ← honest
   ____

2. Brent said he would help his dad clean the garage.

   Because he was in such a hurry, he did a poor job, leaving most of the work for his dad. ← [ ]

   ______________________ ← honest
   ____

3. Kyra found a shiny ring in the sand at the playground.

   She told her mom a friend gave it to her to be sure she would be allowed to keep it. ← [ ]

   ______________________ ← honest
   ____

Name: Date:

Honesty

Find an advertisement that you think deceives readers in a magazine or newspaper. Cut it out and paste it in the box. Then describe why you think it is dishonest.

A Dishonest Advertisement

My Comments:

Name: Date:

Honesty

Ask your family and friends for examples of their honesty. Write them down and answer the question.

Examples of Honesty from My Family and Friends

1. ______________________________

____

2. ______________________________

____

3. ______________________________

____

4. ______________________________

____

Which one of these have you practised recently? Give an example.

____

____

____

____

____

Name: Date:

Generosity

Mack watched while the other kids brought in their gifts for Drew's party. "I don't have anything to give," he thought to himself. "I shouldn't be here."

As the children set their gifts on the table, Mack turned to leave.

"Mack!" came a cry from the other side of the crowd. "You're going the wrong way. The party's just beginning."

"I...I...don't have a gift," said Mack. "I shouldn't have come."

Drew looked from Mack to the gifts on the table and back to Mack. The gifts do not matter, his look said. Mack knew then that he had already given Drew a gift, a gift more valuable than any ribbon-wrapped box in the room: his friendship.

There is more than one kind of gift, and Mack learned this at the party. Mack unknowingly brought a gift for his friend just by being there. He brought himself, his friendship. How much more valuable is a gift that takes time and effort! Like Drew, we should all appreciate this type of gift, whether we are its receivers or its givers.

Name: Date:

Generosity

Only one of each pair of words has a meaning similar to generosity. Circle the similar word. Then write a sentence using the word.

1. ***give*** ***take***

   Sentence: ______________________________

   ____

2. ***share*** ***hoard***

   Sentence: ______________________________

   ____

3. ***stingy*** ***charitable***

   Sentence: ______________________________

   ____

4. 

   Sentence: ______________________________

   ____

   ____

Name: Date:

Generosity

Write a Cinquain poem about generosity. Then read it out to your class.

Form of Cinquain Poem about Generosity

one word → title

two words → describing generosity

three words → generosity in action

four words → express feelings resulting from generosity

one word → another word for generosity

Generosity

________ ________

________ ________ ________

________ ________ ________ ________

____

Name: Date:

Generosity

Just as it is important to be generous, it is important to acknowledge other people's generosity towards us. Look at the pictures. Then answer the questions.

1. How are people generous to you? Give two examples.

- ______________________________
- ______________________________

2. How do you respond when people are generous to you?

____

Name: Date:

Generosity – Part 1

What do you have to give? Give gifts of future time, talent, love, or friendship in the form of a gift certificate. Make your own gift certificates to give to your friends and family.

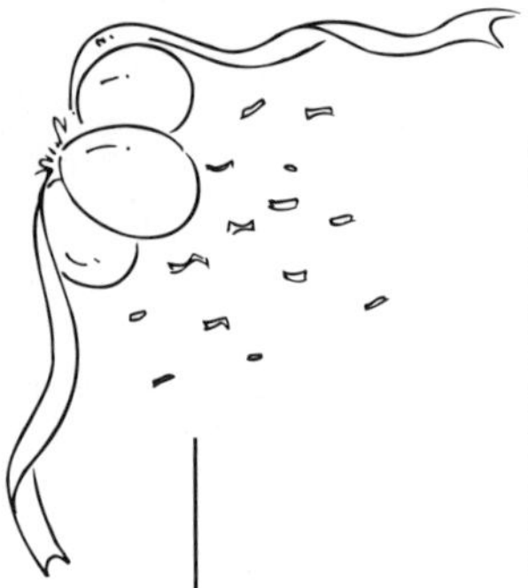

To: ______

Gift of: ______

From: ______

To: ______

Gift of: ______

From: ______

To: ______

Gift of: ______

From: ______

Name: Date:

Generosity – Part 2

Make wrapping paper for your gift certificates. Design your paper in pencil. Then use markers or pencil crayons to colour it. Cut it out, wrap your gift, and send it out to the right person.

Make more wrapping paper by tracing this onto other sheets. Then design and cut them out to wrap the other gift certificates.

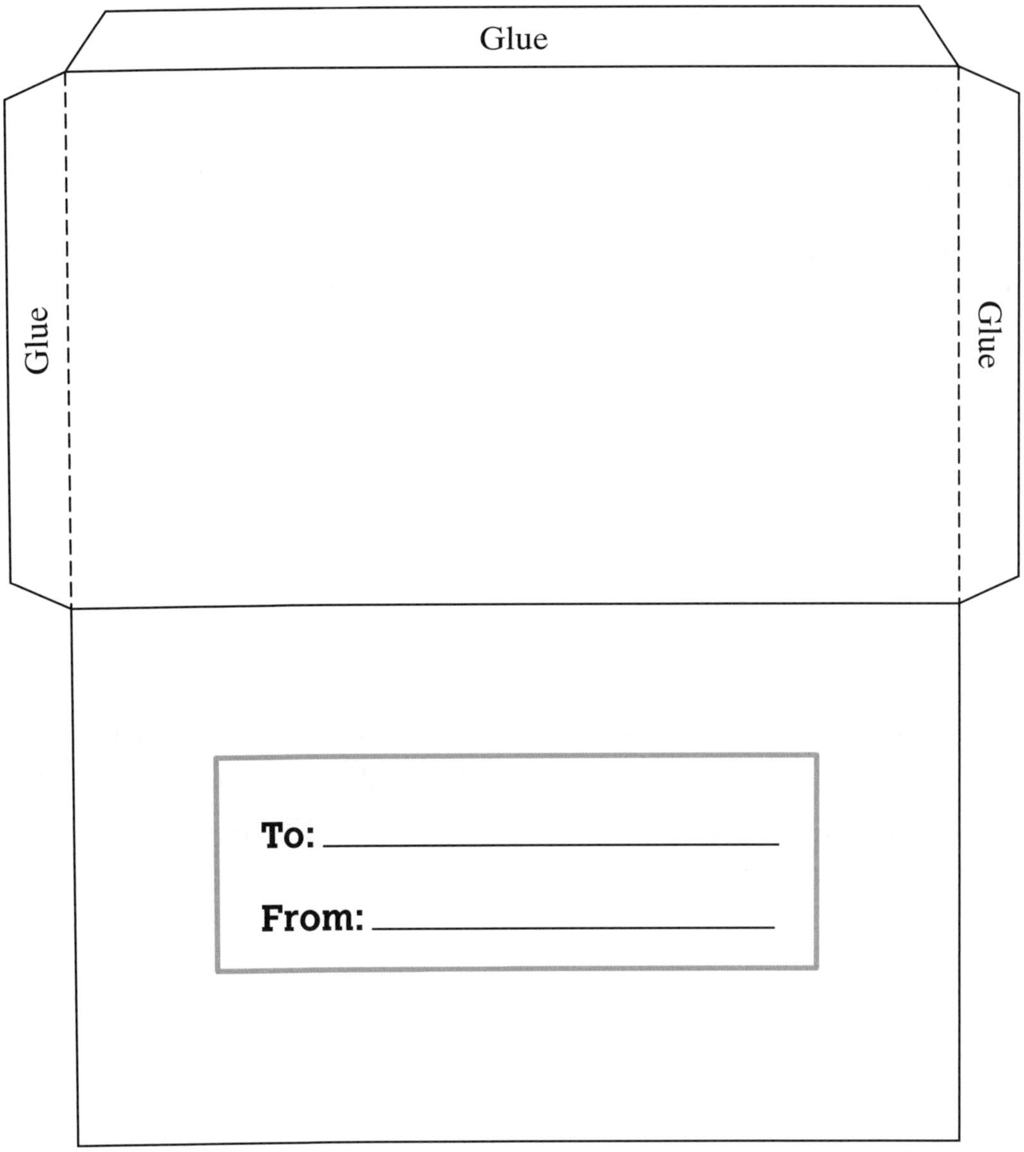

Name: Date:

Respect

Respectful behaviour means treating others as we would like to be treated: kindly and politely. It is following the rules of a particular place while you are there. Respect helps things run smoothly, keeps people safe, and keeps relationships between people healthy.

Name: Date:

Respect

Write a rule you follow on the sign for each of the following places.

One of the ways we show respect is by following the rules of the place we are at.

Name: Date:

Respect

Answer the questions.

Being respected gives us a sense of value. Everybody is valuable, and should be respected, but different people have different ways of showing their respect.

1. How do people show their respect for you?

2. How does it feel?

3. How do people show disrespect for you?

4. How does it feel?

Name: Date:

Respect

Draw and list four people you respect. Then write how you show your respect towards them.

People I Respect

1.
- Who? ______________________
- How? ______________________

____

2.
- Who? ______________________
- How? ______________________

____

3.
- Who? ______________________
- How? ______________________

____

4.
- Who? ______________________
- How? ______________________

____

Name: Date:

Respect

Think about a person that you respect. Draw the person and write what you respect about him or her.

______ is a person that ______

I respect because ______

Name: Date:

Respect

Put a checkmark beside your respectful actions.

____ I follow the rules of the place where I am.

____ I talk respectfully about people, without gossiping.

____ I use polite phrases like "please" and "thank you".

____ I don't call people names.

____ I treat people the way I would like to be treated.

____ I don't laugh at other people's mistakes.

____ I respect myself by getting enough sleep.

____ I respect myself by eating the right foods.

____ I arrive on time for school and other appointments.

If some lines are unchecked, think of what you might do to be a more respectful person.

Name: Date:

Helpfulness

This is the apple that William wanted.

This is the ladder tall and steep that could reach the apple that William wanted.

This is the lad who climbed the ladder tall and steep that reached the apple that William wanted.

This is the gal who fetched the lad who climbed the ladder that reached the apple that William wanted.

This is why William wanted the apple.

William was able to help the horse, but only with the help of the ladder, the lad, and the gal. They all helped each other to give the horse a juicy treat.

Helpfulness is something we ask for from others and give to others.

Name: Date:

Helpfulness

Some people are helpful to others as part of their jobs. Write a sentence that describes how each of these people helps others.

1.

2.

3.

4.

5.

6.

Name: Date:

Helpfulness

Give examples to show how you are helpful at home and at school. Then name another place where you are helpful and write how you are helpful there, too.

How are you helpful to others

at home?

at school?

Name: Date:

Helpfulness

One way to be helpful is to do chores at home. Keep track of your chores and your helpfulness with this chore table for one month. Write the chores you did in the boxes.

Chores at Home

- dishes
- laundry
- making my bed
- watering plants
- sweeping floors
- vacuuming
- mopping

	Sunday	Monday	Tuesday	Wednesday	Thursday	Friday	Saturday
Week 1							
Week 2							
Week 3							
Week 4							
Week 5							

Name: Date:

Helpfulness

When do you need help? Who helps you? Give examples.

Sometimes we need help. It is important to know that asking for help is not a sign of weakness.

I need help when...	The one who helps me is...

Name: Date:

Helpfulness

Hands are often used as symbols for helpfulness. Draw outlines of your hand and the hands of your friends. Link them together as a symbol of how you help one another.

Our Hands

Name: Date:

Perseverance

SUNDAY NEWS

Girl Finds Lost Dog Against All Odds

There was almost no chance Amanda Brown would ever find her missing pooch. At least, that was what her family, her teacher, her friends, and even the local animal shelter told her.

But Amanda does not give up easily and, fortunately for her dog, her perseverance paid off.

After two weeks and over a hundred missing dog posters later, a jogger recognized a tired and cold dog as the one he had seen on Amanda's poster.

Amanda persevered in looking for her missing dog. Long after most people would have given up, Amanda's perseverance paid off and her dog was not only found, but probably saved!

Perseverance does not always pay off in such a remarkable way, but it is always good to know we have tried our best at something and did not give up.

Name: Date:

Perseverance

Draw lines to connect the words that are related to perseverance to the climber.

- persistence
- endurance
- impatience
- commitment
- diligence
- distracted
- determined
- uncommitted
- stamina
- patience
- sloppy
- lazy

Name: Date:

Perseverance

Think of difficulties you have overcome, as well as difficulties you will need to overcome, to achieve something you want.

Things I have done that required perseverance:

1. ____________________

2. ____________________

3. ____________________

Goals I have that require perseverance:

1. ____________________

2. ____________________

3. ____________________

Name: Date:

Perseverance

Find a headline from a newspaper that tells a true story of perseverance. Cut it out and paste the headline below. Illustrate the story.

Name: Date:

Perseverance

Some words and phrases encourage us to persevere. Colour those phrases to find the path to success.

Name: Date:

Perseverance

Put a checkmark on the line if you agree with the sentence.

Do you have perseverance?

____ I am not afraid to try new things just because they seem difficult.

____ I make goals and try to stick to them.

____ I work towards my goals every day.

____ I do not give up when the going gets tough.

____ I learn from my mistakes.

____ I am patient with myself.

____ I look ahead towards what could be, rather than see only what is happening now.

____ I seek help from others when I need it.

If most of the lines have checkmarks, you are probably a persevering person.

Name: Date:

Tolerance

People are different from one another in many ways. People of different cultures speak different languages, celebrate different holidays, and eat different foods. People of different cultures may also have different customs and wear different clothes. No matter how many differences we have, there are always things we have in common.

The more we learn about differences, the more we understand them. The more we understand, the more tolerance we have. It is important that people learn about their differences. Sometimes it is through examining our differences that we also see how we are the same.

Name: Date:

Tolerance

Find the word that fits the definition to complete the puzzle.

an idea we have about people that is not based on facts

knowing enough about something so that we can appreciate it

the belief we have about something

acceptance of differences in opinions and ways of living

unfair treatment

unflattering and harmful beliefs about people based on their race

the mistaken idea that everyone of a certain group is the same

a rigid opinion about a person or group of people

lack of knowledge or understanding

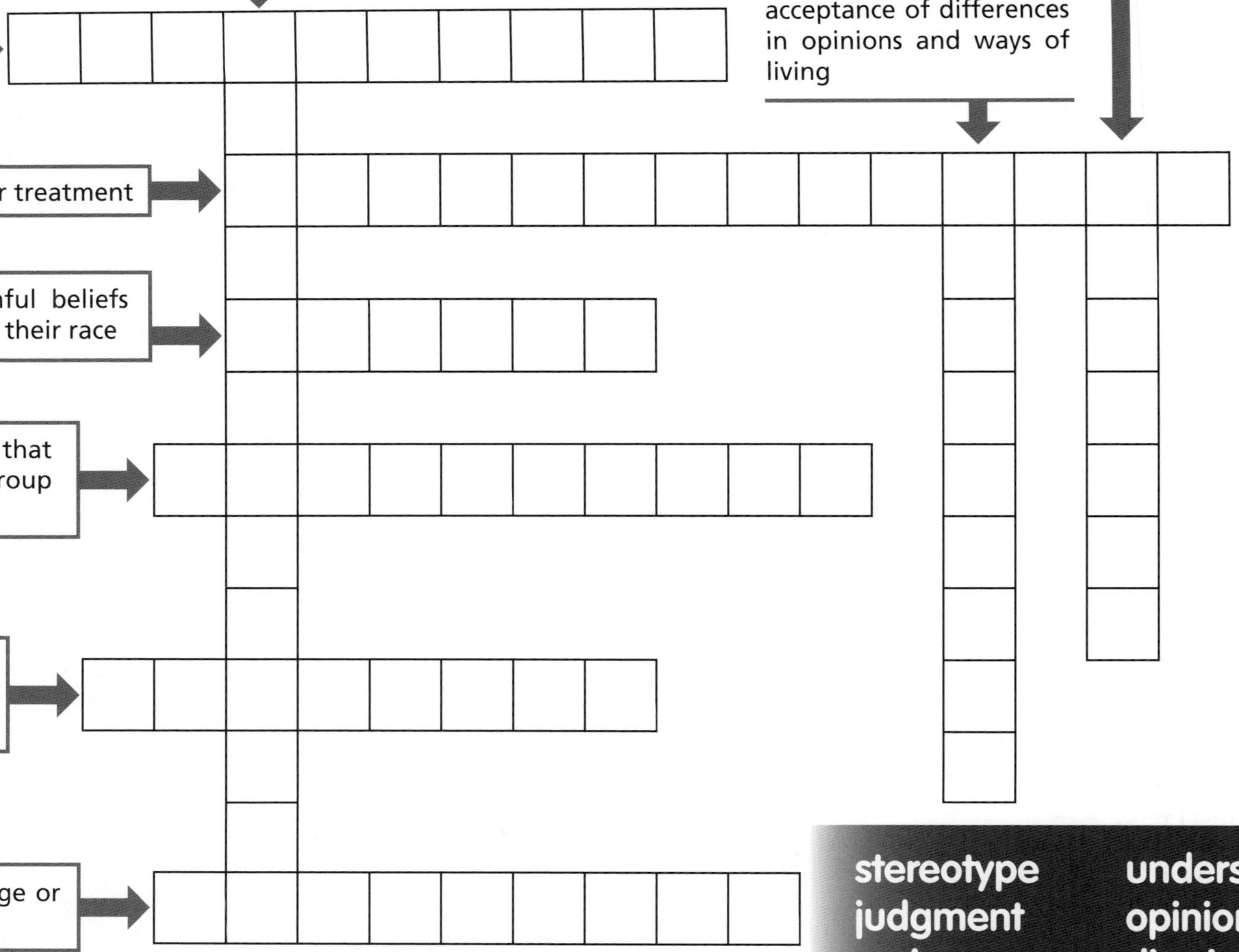

stereotype
judgment
racism
assumption
tolerance
understanding
opinion
discrimination
ignorance

Name: Date:

Tolerance

How well do you know these stereotypes? Fill in the blanks. Then answer the questions.

Stereotypes do not promote tolerance. They prevent us from seeing individuals for who they are, and are often hurtful.

1. All ____________________ like cooking.
2. All ____________________ are careless.
3. All ____________________ love hockey.

How many more stereotypes can you list?

4. ____________________
5. ____________________
6. ____________________

Have you ever been considered a stereotype? If so, how did it feel? How is stereotyping a form of intolerance?

____

____

____

Name: Date:

Tolerance

Find somebody who is different from you in each of the following ways. Then write one thing that you and that person have in common.

1. 

Family Structure: ________________ and I are different.

Things we have in common: ________________

2. 

Skin Colour: ________________ and I are different.

Things we have in common: ________________

3. 

Favourite Music: ________________ and I are different.

Things we have in common: ________________

4. 

Birth Country: ________________ and I are different.

Things we have in common: ________________

5. 

Mother Tongue: ________________ and I are different.

Things we have in common: ________________

Name: Date:

Tolerance

Colour the bars to measure your tolerance.

My Tolerance

(self-evaluation)

1. I appreciate differences among people.

never always

2. I embrace other people's ways of doing things.

never always

3. I enjoy being friends with people who are different from me without judging them.

never always

4. I accept the ideas and customs of people who are different from me.

never always

Name: Date:

Tolerance

Draw a picture of yourself and someone who is different from you. Write sentences to describe what makes you and your friend unique.

Someone I know

Myself

Name: Date:

Self-discipline

James and Isabella's Chores (I)

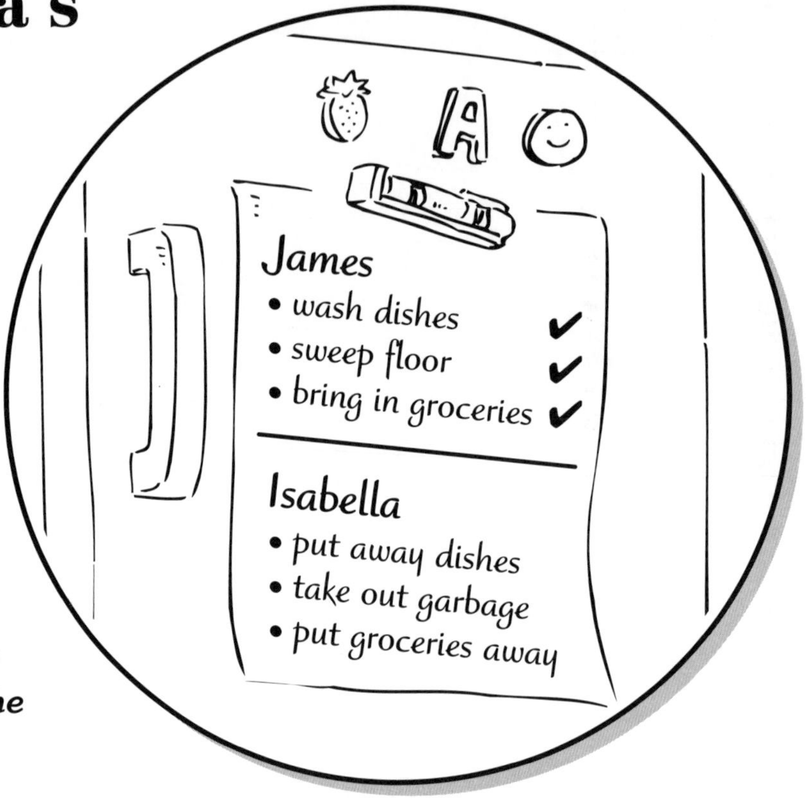

On Saturday morning, James did his chores. He washed the dishes, swept the floor, and brought in all the groceries.

Then he went out to play.

Isabella slept in and did not do her chores. She did not put away the dishes. She did not take out the garbage. And she did not put the groceries away.

When Isabella woke up, she went out to play.

The day was hot, and soon Mom called, "Isabella and James, it's time for ice cream!"

In the kitchen, Mom could not find the ice cream scoop. She said, "Who forgot to put away the dishes James washed?"

"Oops," said Isabella. "I didn't put them away." Isabella washed the ice cream scoop, but then Mom saw the overflowing garbage can.

"Who forgot to take out the garbage James filled?" asked Mom.

"Oops," said Isabella. "I didn't take it out." They all plugged their noses, but then Mom saw the grocery bags on the table.

Name: Date:

Self-discipline

James and Isabella's Chores (II)

"Oops," said Isabella. "I didn't put the groceries away." But it was too late for Isabella to put them away. She took out the box of melted ice cream and put it in the garbage.

Then she took the garbage out.

James showed self-discipline when he did his chores before playing.

Because Isabella did not do her chores at the right time – and did not show self-discipline – she and James did not get their ice cream treat on a hot day.

Self-discipline is doing the things we are supposed to do, even if it is easier or more fun to do otherwise. It could be doing something like chores or homework, or it could be behaving well even when we are tired or angry.

When we have self-discipline, we are in control of our own actions and feelings.

Name: Date:

Self-discipline

Read the situations that test your self-discipline. Write what you would do in each situation.

1. The answers to the questions on the test are right in front of you. You know you should not cheat, but everyone else is doing it. What do you do?

2. It is your job to rake the leaves from the front yard, and you are half finished. Your friend has invited you to a movie that starts in ten minutes. He is waiting for your answer. What do you do?

3. Your sister lost all the ride tickets at the fair. You will not get to ride the roller coaster, and you are angry! What do you do?

Name: Date:

Self-discipline

Answer the questions and draw a picture to show how you felt.

1. Can you think of something you did that did not show self-discipline? Write about it.

____

____

____

2. What were the consequences of your lack of self-discipline?

____

____

3. How did it make you feel?

____

____

____

4. 

What should you have done to show self-discipline?

____

____

____

Name: Date:

Self-discipline

Find the words related to self-discipline below. Write them on the lines. Then cut out the bottom part of this paper and pin it somewhere as a reminder to be self-disciplined.

Some of the characteristics will help us show self-discipline, while others will be the result of our self-discipline.

diligence responsibility patience laziness

bias trustworthiness reliability blame

tolerance determination unhelpfulness self-motivation

perseverance destruction cooperativeness moderation

resourcefulness dependency violence politeness

untrustworthiness punctuality commitment narrow-mindedness

Self-discipline

Name: Date:

Self-discipline

What goal do you have that will take self-discipline to achieve? Draw a picture of you reaching that goal.

Sometimes our goals are difficult to reach because they take so much self-discipline.

I do my homework without being reminded. I am a self-disciplined person.

My Goal

Name: Date:

Patience

Patience is the ability to wait for something without anger or irritation.

There are many times when we must wait: in grocery store lineups, for a favourite TV show to come on, or for water to boil. Being patient makes time pass more enjoyably.

There are times when we don't need to wait but should. If we wait for a friend to catch up on the way to school, we are rewarded with someone to walk with. Waiting for the light to turn green before we cross the street is worthwhile because it keeps us safe. Having patience makes it easier to wait.

We also use patience in our dealings with others. Showing patience with others is kind and tolerant. And if we are patient with others, they are more likely to be patient with us.

Name: Date:

Patience

For each picture, write a sentence to explain who is being patient and why you think the picture shows this.

People who are patient:

1 ______________________________

____

2 ______________________________

____

3 ______________________________

____

4 ______________________________

____

Name: Date:

Patience

Complete the chart with words to compare your feelings and actions when you are patient with how you feel when you are impatient.

	when I am patient	when I am impatient
How I feel		
How I act		

Name: Date:

Patience

Answer these questions.

1. When is it easiest for me to be patient?

2. When is it most difficult for me to be patient?

3. When do I need to be more patient?

4. Who is patient with me?

5. How can I be more patient?

Name: Date:

Patience

Find the words related to patience. Write them on the bookmark. Then decorate the bookmark and cut it out so that you can keep it in your agenda.

perseverance lazy kindness
tolerance urgent respect
impatient cooperation commitment
negative critical generous
helpful discouraging untrustworthy
loyalty unfaithful timid
self-control narrow-minded

Name: Date:

Patience

Read the story and answer the questions.

Jenny and Winnie were waiting for their dad to come home to take them to a movie. Winnie stared at the clock and said, "Jenny, should we call Daddy to remind him the movie starts at 7 p.m.?" Jenny looked at Winnie and replied, "I think you called him already, and all of us know when the movie starts. I am sure Daddy is on his way home; traffic might be keeping him." Jenny took a sip of her drink and continued to read her favourite book. Winnie fought hard to sit on the big, comfy couch. She walked to the window and looked outside to see whether she could see her daddy's car in the distance. She tapped the window over and over, faster and faster, to release her temper.

Finally, their dad arrived home at 6:40 p.m., and he was sure they would make it to the movie on time. Jenny greeted her dad cheerfully and put on her jacket to get ready for the movie. But their dad found that Winnie was frustrated and furious. He asked Winnie, "What happened, sweetie?"

1. Which girl showed patience?

____

2. How did she make good use of her time while she was waiting?

____

3. Do you think doing something to distract yourself from the things that you are waiting for helps you to be more patient? Why?

____

____

4. Share an experience you have had where you demonstrated patience.

____

____

Name: Date:

Loyalty

Loyalty is...

A dog who's there no matter what,

Who greets me every day.

A friend who is still a friend tomorrow,

Though I couldn't play today.

Loyalty is one of the ways we show closeness to a person or thing. We are loyal to our families and to our friends, showing our loyalty by supporting a person through bad times as well as good.

Organizations and places gain strength through people's loyalty. A business, a school, or even a country is healthier when people are loyal to it.

Name: Date:

Loyalty

Read what Sam says. Answer the questions.

How do you show loyalty to your school?

1. ______________________________
2. ______________________________
3. ______________________________
4. ______________________________

What other ways could you show loyalty to your school?

1. ______________________________
2. ______________________________
3. ______________________________
4. ______________________________

Name: Date:

Loyalty

We can show loyalty to a product, business, or organization, as well as to people.

Fill in the missing words to find ways we show loyalty. Then write a sentence to share your experience.

1. 

remembering ____________________ with a card or a phone call

My Experience ____

2. 

buying the ____________________ when it works well for us

My Experience ____

3. 

frequenting the ____________________ because it gives great service

My Experience ____

4. 

wearing ____________________ at a game

My Experience ____

Name: Date:

Loyalty

Answer these questions about loyalty.

1. a. Who are you loyal to?

b. Why are you loyal to them?

2. a. Should we show loyalty to everyone equally?

b. Why or why not?

3.

Are there some people we should not be loyal to? Why?

Name: Date:

Loyalty

Give examples of people, places, and commitments that you are loyal to.

People (family, friends, etc.):

I am loyal to ______________________________

I show my loyalty by ______________________________

____

Place (school, country, etc.):

I am loyal to ______________________________

I show my loyalty by ______________________________

____

Commitment (goal, chore, plan, etc.):

I am loyal to ______________________________

I show my loyalty by ______________________________

____

Name: Date:

Loyalty

Draw a picture of your loyal friend wearing the crown. Colour the picture. Then write how your friend showed his or her loyalty.

My Loyal Friend

Name: Date:

Forgiveness

When people commit an injustice against us – step on our toe or call us names, for example – we may feel angry towards them. If they are genuinely sorry for their misdeed, it is important that we quickly forgive. Anger in this case only hurts us more.

Sometimes we can't be sure that someone is sorry for what they have done. It is still good to be able to forgive. When we can go forward in our lives without bad feelings towards another, everybody benefits.

How do we show forgiveness? One way is by moving on and not dwelling on the offence or mistake. Another way is to say, "I forgive you." Saying "I forgive you" can be as difficult as saying "I'm sorry." But do not worry. They will be welcome words!

Name: Date:

Forgiveness

Think about times when you have forgiven and been forgiven. Then answer the questions.

1. How do you feel when someone does something to hurt you, whether by accident or on purpose?

____

____

2. How do you feel when the person apologizes?

____

____

3. How do you feel when you forgive that person?

____

____

4. How do you think the person feels when he or she is forgiven?

____

____

Name: Date:

Forgiveness

Forgiveness involves the understanding that everyone makes mistakes. Read what Julia says and answer the questions.

Remembering our own mistakes and imperfections helps if we are having trouble forgiving someone.

Make a list of times you have wanted forgiveness for something you did.

1. ______________________________
2. ______________________________
3. ______________________________
4. ______________________________

How do you feel when you are forgiven for doing something wrong?

____

____

Why do you think people need forgiveness?

____

____

Name: Date:

Forgiveness

There are many feelings and actions that can lead us to be forgiving. Find and circle the words in the word search.

fair self-control gracious patient tolerant
considerate generous cheerful sympathetic kindness
cooperative understanding listening

s	q	n	t	e	n	t	d	h	i	n	g	i	o	u	s
y	f	h	a	d	f	z	x	f	a	i	r	s	c	f	e
t	v	r	s	b	q	c	v	l	h	y	a	r	o	k	g
e	i	l	x	q	f	k	j	i	a	n	c	o	n	i	e
h	k	i	n	d	n	e	s	s	t	s	i	m	s	t	n
o	t	o	l	e	r	a	n	t	e	w	o	e	i	g	e
i	g	f	b	o	c	h	e	e	r	f	u	l	d	s	r
a	s	u	l	y	p	a	e	n	t	u	s	o	e	n	o
c	o	o	p	e	r	a	t	i	v	e	p	u	r	t	u
j	k	e	p	a	t	i	e	n	t	f	l	k	a	o	s
w			w	g	d	a	n	g	o	b	j	s	t	o	g
			y	f	s	t	e	n	t	i	n	g	e	f	n
		s	e	l	f	-	c	o	n	t	r	o	l	r	y
	k	o	u	n	d	e	r	s	t	a	n	d	i	n	g
	j	t	h	s	y	m	p	a	t	h	e	t	i	c	e
	p	s	r	e	a	n	t	s	g	r	b	e	t	f	a

Name: Date:

Forgiveness

Use this page to make a collage of pictures and words that indicate forgiveness is needed. Use headlines and pictures from old magazines or newspapers. Then check the sentences describing the benefits of forgiveness.

FORGIVENESS

- ◯ Understand that everybody makes mistakes.
- ◯ Look to the future instead of the past.
- ◯ Admit that nobody is perfect, not even you.
- ◯ Get rid of feelings of frustration and anger.

Name: Date:

Forgiveness

Write an "I forgive you" letter for one of the following characters.

A From: the Three Bears
To: Goldilocks

B From: Little Miss Muffet
To: the Spider

Dear ________________ ,

____

____

____

____

____

____

____

____

With love,

Name: Date:

Reliability

Melissa relies on Jane because Jane is a reliable person.

Being reliable means being someone that others can depend on.

Do you brush your teeth before bed? Do you do your chores and your homework? If you do, you are being reliable, and it helps your teacher and your family, but most of all, it helps you.

It takes effort to be reliable. Reliability does not just happen. What if you are counted on to be somewhere but another, better, opportunity comes up? Do you stick with your first responsibility, or abandon it for the new opportunity? Reliable people stick with the first, even if it means they cannot do the second.

Name: Date:

Reliability

A. Make a list of ways to be reliable.

1. ______________________

   ____

2. ______________________

   ____

3. ______________________

4. ______________________

B. List two areas of your life where you could be more reliable. Write what you can do to be more reliable.

1. **One area** where I could be more reliable is ______________________

I can be more reliable by ______________________

____

2. **Another area** where I could be more reliable is ______________________

I can be more reliable by ______________________

____

Name: Date:

Reliability

Write a haiku about the reliability of something in nature.

Many things in nature are reliable. One example is the seasons – summer follows spring, which follows winter and fall. Another is the constellations in the night sky; the stars form the same familiar patterns night after night. They are reliable.

Quick Reference

A haiku is a sparsely worded poem. Non-rhyming, it has the following format:

1st line	5 syllables
2nd line	7 syllables
3rd line	5 syllables

Name: Date:

Reliability

Read the story. Then answer the questions.

The Woodbine Community supported a program called "Love our Earth" and welcomed all students to participate. This program was designed to show students how to preserve our Earth by planting. Each of the participants was given a small potted plant. If the participant brought back a healthy plant after a month, he or she got a prize.

Joseph, Elaine, and Andy participated in this program. Joseph brought a plant home, and decided to give it to his mother. Joseph said, "Mom, I am busy with my homework. Can you help me take care of this plant for a month?"

Elaine kept her plant by the window, but she forgot to give it water for almost three weeks. When Elaine checked the plant, she said, "Oh no! I don't think it's alive."

Andy placed his plant on a windowsill and created a schedule reminding himself to water it every four days. He checked his agenda every night to make sure nothing was missing.

After a month, successful participants proudly brought their plants to the community centre to get a prize. Andy's plant was the healthiest and the strongest!

1. Colour the bars to show the children's reliability.

Reliability

	least	moderate	most
Joseph			
Elaine			
Andy			

2. Does this story help you understand why it is important to be a reliable person? If yes, how?

Name: Date:

Reliability

Write down your regular weekly commitments on the schedule. Decorate your schedule. Then cut it out and keep it where you will see it every day.

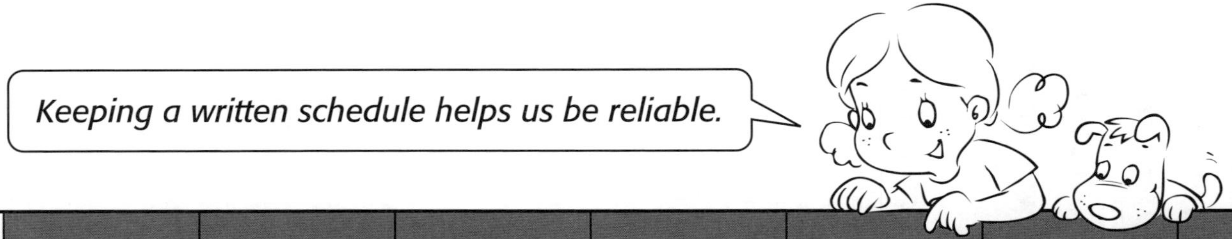

My Schedule	SUNDAY	MONDAY	TUESDAY	WEDNESDAY	THURSDAY	FRIDAY	SATURDAY
7:00 a.m.							
8:00 a.m.							
9:00 a.m.							
10:00 a.m.							
11:00 a.m.							
12:00 p.m.							
1:00 p.m.							
2:00 p.m.							
3:00 p.m.							
4:00 p.m.							
5:00 p.m.							
6:00 p.m.							
7:00 p.m.							
8:00 p.m.							
9:00 p.m.							

Name: Date:

Reliability

Put a checkmark beside each sentence that describes you.

Reliability Checklist

____ I get to school on time.

____ I arrive home on time.

____ I get my homework done on time.

____ I put toys and books away when I am finished with them.

____ I do my chores.

____ I return things I borrow.

____ I am loyal to my friends.

____ I ask permission before taking or using something that does not belong to me.

____ I am helpful.

____ I keep my promises.

Colour the correct number of boxes to match the number of checkmarks shown above to see your reliability.

My Reliability

least — most

Name: Date:

Commitment

To have commitment to something is to be dedicated to it. We commit to tasks or jobs that we agree to do. Parents are committed to their families, as are families to their pets. These commitments ensure that all members of the family are taken care of. We show responsibility when we keep our commitments.

We should all be committed to ourselves. When we eat healthy foods and exercise, we show commitment to ourselves. Any way we take care of ourselves, from paying attention in class to trying to be good people, shows commitment.

Besides being committed to our families and friends, we can be committed to other things. Being committed helps us reach our goals.

Name: Date:

Commitment

Draw a line to match the commitment with one of the pictures depicting the effort it takes to stay committed.

Commitment to...

walk neighbours' dog while they are on holidays •

learn how to play the piano •

foster kittens for the SPCA •

conserving energy •

the swim team •

Name: Date:

Commitment

Read the story. Then write about an experience where you demonstrated each of the three character traits by keeping your commitment.

1. **Responsibility and Commitment**

2. **Determination and Commitment**

3. **Trustworthiness and Commitment**

Name: Date:

Commitment

Answer these questions.

1.

Write about something you are committed to for your family. What is it?

Why are you committed to it? Is it a difficult commitment to keep? If so, in what way?

2.

Write about something you are committed to for yourself. What is it?

Why are you committed to it? Is it a difficult commitment to keep? If so, in what way?

Name: Date:

Commitment

Draw a picture of yourself doing something you are committed to doing. Write your plan for keeping your commitment.

Commitment ______________________________

____

____

____

Name: Date:

Commitment

Make a Pledge of Commitment to yourself. Ask your parents or teacher to sign it for you. Then cut it out and post it in your bedroom.

Pledge of Commitment

I, ______________________, pledge to

____

____

Signed ______________________ Witness ______________________

Dated ______________________ Dated ______________________

Name: Date:

Friendliness

Fred's Friends (I)

One day when Fred was walking downtown, he had a funny feeling that he was all alone.

It was very strange, for people were all around him. Old Sid was just behind him, sitting on a bench. And there was Madeleine, shopping with her mother. Mr. Leung was busy sweeping in front of his store.

But Fred could not see beyond his own nose, and he was quite certain he was alone. He started to search for his friends.

When people saw Fred peering under bushes and peeking behind trees, they asked, "What are you looking for, Fred?"

Sid noticed Fred and said, "Come on over to my house, Fred. We can visit, and it will take your mind off whatever you've lost."

Name: Date:

Friendliness

Fred's Friends (II)

"Let me help you look, Fred," said Madeleine. "You're always around when I need help."

Madeleine's mother also piped in, "Good luck, Fred! I hope you find what you're looking for."

Even busy Mr. Leung noticed Fred. "Hi, Fred!" he said. "I can't help you look now, but if you can't find it, come by the store and maybe I can replace it for you."

Suddenly Fred felt foolish. He didn't lose his friends at all. He was surrounded by friendly people.

Sometimes it is good to be alone, but even when we're alone, it is nice to know we have friends. Fred found out that even people that were not his friends – maybe people just passing him on the street – were friendly towards him, and could be his friends.

Friendliness is not just for friends. We are friendly to people when we help them or smile at them. We are friendly to kids on our soccer team, even if we barely know them, when we are kind to them.

We should extend friendliness to people whether they are our friends or not.

Name: Date:

Friendliness

Think about friendliness between you and your friends, and friendliness you share with people you do not know well. Answer the questions to understand what is different between the two, if anything is.

1. How do people who do not know you show friendliness to you?

2. How do you show friendliness to them?

3. How do people who know you well show friendliness to you?

4. How do you show friendliness to them?

Name: Date:

Friendliness

Finish the sentences below to know what kind of friend you are. Then answer the question.

What Kind of Friend Are You?

1. When my friend needs help, I ______________________________

____

2. When my friend is sad, I ______________________________

____

3. When my friend and I disagree, I ______________________________

____

4. When my friend and I are with other friends, I ______________________________

____

What do you think is meant by the saying, "A friend in need is a friend indeed"?

____

____

____

____

____

Name: Date:

Friendliness

Draw a picture of yourself and your friends. Then answer the questions.

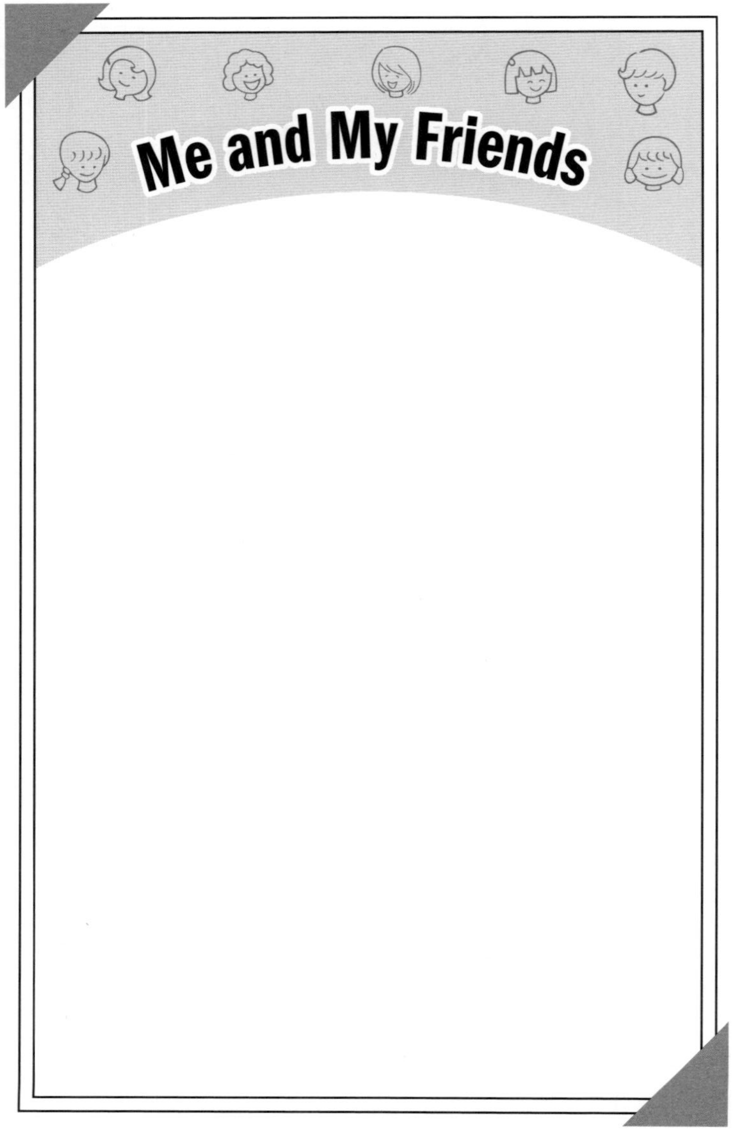

List the things you enjoy doing with your friends.

1. ______________________________

____

2. ______________________________

____

3. ______________________________

____

What qualities do you look for in a friend?
(Check the circles.)

❍ trustful	❍ kind	❍ flexible
❍ helpful	❍ fair	❍ reliable
❍ thankful	❍ honest	❍ patient
❍ cheerful	❍ loyal	❍ generous

Name: Date:

Friendliness

Make a bookmark for each of your friends. On each bookmark, write the quality that you like most about that friend. Decorate the bookmark. Then cut it out and give it to your friend.

To: ____________

I like you most ...

From: ____________

Thank you for being my friend!

To: ____________

From: ____________

To: ____________

Your Special Character ____________

From: ____________

Name: Date:

Responsibility

Teacher: ***Who will be responsible for the gerbil's afternoon feeding?***

Ryan: ***I can do it.***

Teacher: ***Great! You will feed the gerbil every day at afternoon recess.***

Ryan: ***But, what about playing outside?***

Teacher: ***Well, first take care of your new responsibility, and then join the others outside.***

Ryan thought about what his teacher said. He loved to play outside at recess, but he also liked the idea of having a responsibility. He would be responsible, he thought, and feed the gerbil every afternoon. He sat up taller, proud that he had volunteered for this responsibility.

Responsibility is a big word in more ways than one. Taking on new responsibilities can be hard, especially when the responsibility may interfere with other things we like to do.

For Ryan, the responsibility of taking care of the gerbil means having a shorter recess. After thinking about it, though, he is okay with it. He knows that having a responsibility will teach him more about responsibility. If he does a good job, people will notice. He may even earn new, even more rewarding responsibilities.

Name: Date:

Responsibility

These words are related to responsibility. Which word best describes each event? Write the word in the box. Then describe an experience you have had where you demonstrated that trait.

duty **obligation** **reliability**

1. [ ]

- *I am one of the members of my family, so I need to keep our house clean and tidy.*

- ______________________________

2. [ ]

- Everyone likes Joseph because he always keeps his promises.
- ______________________________

3. [ ]

- Katie brings the attendance record to the office every Monday.
- ______________________________

Name: Date:

Responsibility

For each situation, check the responsible answer.

1. Grandma bought you a new pair of ice skates.

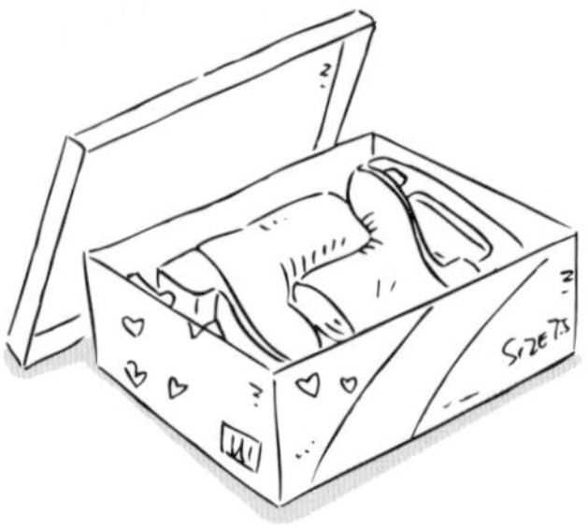

Ⓐ You put them in your skating bag and send her a thank-you letter.

Ⓑ You leave them on the front porch until you are ready to use them.

Ⓒ You send her a thank-you letter, but store them under your bed because you don't like skating anymore.

2. You now have three pairs of ice skates, but only your new ones from Grandma fit you properly.

Ⓐ You throw away your old skates – they don't fit anyway.

Ⓑ You start a new old-skate collection to put beside your old-winter-jacket collection.

Ⓒ You donate your old skates to charity.

3. It's your job to wash dishes, and just as you are washing the last one, your dad puts his used popcorn bowl beside the sink.

Ⓐ You insist that it's your dad's job to wash the popcorn bowl – he's the one that used it.

Ⓑ You wash his popcorn bowl and feel proud that every dish in the kitchen is clean.

Ⓒ You finish the dish you are washing but leave the popcorn bowl – whoever washes the dishes in the morning will have to do it.

Name: Date:

Responsibility

A woman with a cane is about to go into a store, and she accidentally drops her hanky. Look at the child's response in each picture. Put the pictures in order from the one depicting the least responsible action to the one depicting the most.

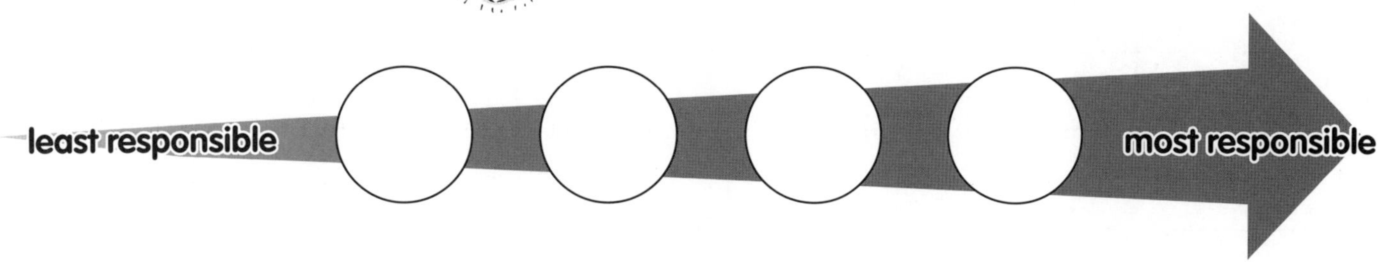

Name: Date:

Responsibility

Read Gretchen's "Things To Do" list. Write out your own list of things you are responsible for today.

Things To Do

- make bed
- brush teeth
- feed fish
- water plants
- make dentist appointment
- accept Megan's birthday party invitation
- write thank-you letter to Grandma

Things to Do

Name: Date:

Responsibility

Read what Mrs. Armstrong says. Then draw a picture that shows what one of your important responsibilities is and describe it.

Different people take on different responsibilities in their lives depending on their interests and concerns. A police officer has different responsibilities from a school teacher. Someone who is concerned about the environment will take on different responsibilities from someone who feels strongly about the safety of astronauts in space.

My Responsibility

Name: Date:

Courage

In the first headline, the boy's courage is obvious. He must have faced great danger to save his friend from an alligator. This is often the type of story about courage that makes headlines, but there are many more acts of courage that happen every day and are never reported.

For example, we would never see the second headline. Susie's act was not dangerous. It was not even unusual. But it was an act of courage. There are many other situations like this one. Talking to someone new, trying something new, or standing up to a bully can all be acts of courage.

Name: Date:

Courage

Read what Joseph says. Then answer the questions.

1. Describe something you did that took courage.

2.

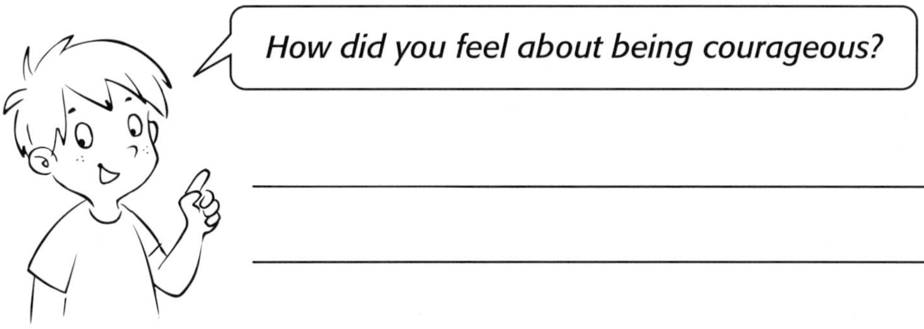

Name: Date:

Courage

Complete the picture of the superhero by drawing your likeness in his costume. Then write two or three sentences to describe how brave your superhero is.

My Superhero

Name: Date:

Courage

Answer the questions so that you can understand more about your courage.

All of us have times when we wish we had more courage. We are all unique in our need for courage because we are all unique in our fears and weaknesses.

1. 
Where do you need to have more courage?

2. 
When do you need to have more courage?

3. 
What can you do to muster up more courage?

Name: Date:

Courage

Change the headlines to show real bravery.

Name: Date:

Courage

Find pictures and words that depict courage from magazines or newspapers. Cut them out and paste them onto this page. Then share your feelings about courage.

People Showing Courage

My Feelings

Name: Date:

Creativity

Creativity is using your imagination to come up with something new, or to solve a problem.

Creativity can be simple, and something you do every day, like these kids looking at clouds.

Creativity is useful for solving problems, and it helps make us unique. The last gardener below is certainly creative in his choice of location for his garden, and it solves the problem of not having enough sun inside his apartment!

Name: Date:

Creativity

Match the words connected to creativity with the definitions. Write the answers on the lines.

clever	inventive	adaptable	imagination	vision
unique	inspiration	creativity	original	resourceful

1. ____________ : skilled or talented
2. ____________ : one of a kind
3. ____________ : the first of its kind
4. ____________ : a view of what might be
5. ____________ : able to create something new
6. ____________ : able to change when needed
7. ____________ : something that encourages creativity
8. ____________ : use of imagination to create something new
9. ____________ : able to find unique ways of using resources
10. ____________ : ideas formed in our head, without the five senses

Name: Date:

Creativity

Think of two different solutions to each problem. Write your solutions.

1. How can the children share when there is only one fancy winter coat?

Solution 1 ____________________

____

____

Solution 2 ____________________

____

____

2. How can the children decide how to spend their recess together?

Solution 1 ____________________

____

____

Solution 2 ____________________

____

____

Name: Date:

Creativity

Answer the questions to explore your creativity.

1. In what ways are you most creative?
(Check the appropriate circles and give an example that you have demonstrated.)

❍ think of a new game to play with friends

❍ create a useful tool to help people

❍ write an interesting story

❍ decorate your bedroom

❍ plant flowers in your backyard

❍ create a new snack with Mom

Example: ____________________

2. What helps you be at your most creative?

____

____

____

3. What keeps you creative at all times?

____

____

____

Name: Date:

Creativity

Cut the pages to make a diary. Take it and a pencil wherever you go.

Keep a diary of your creative ideas. They can be for problem-solving, drawing, creative plans, story ideas, etc.

Idea Diary

Name: Date:

Creativity

Use the checklist to see how creative you are and how open to creativity you are.

Creativity Checklist

____ I try to find solutions to problems.

____ I use my imagination when I create something new.

____ I make up stories, whether written or spoken.

____ I draw pictures.

____ I create my own music.

____ I explore new things that interest me.

____ I write down my ideas when they come to me.

____ I am not afraid to express my ideas.

____ I take time for myself to think.

____ I don't give up easily.

Name: Date:

Thankfulness

Thankfulness is the feeling and expression of appreciation. We can be thankful for events that happened in our lives, for the things we have and the people we know, and for things people do for us.

When we think of expressing thankfulness, we usually think of the words "thank you". They are important words, and we should use them often. But when we are simply thankful for what we have, we show our thanks by being happy. People who appreciate the good things they have in their lives, no matter how little, are usually happy people.

Name: Date:

Thankfulness

Write a list of all the things you are thankful for. Then answer the questions.

I am thankful for...

- ____________________
- ____________________
- ____________________
- ____________________
- ____________________
- ____________________
- ____________________

____

Write why you are thankful for two of the things on your list.

1. I am thankful for ____________________ because ____________________

2. ____________________ because ____________________

Name: Date:

Thankfulness

There are many different ways to show thankfulness. Colour and cut out the petals with the words that show thankfulness. Then glue them onto the flower to make a "thankful" flower.

- credit
- appreciate
- selfish
- patience
- recognize
- acknowledge
- reciprocate
- return favour
- gratitude
- narrow-minded

Name: Date:

Thankfulness

Write notes of appreciation for some of the things you are thankful for. Cut on the lines and give the notes to the people you are thanking.

Colour or decorate them to make them even more beautiful!

Name: Date:

Thankfulness

Write about the people who showed thankfulness towards you. Then answer the question.

Who: ______________________

How he/she showed thanks: ______________________

How it made me feel: ______________________

Who: ______________________

How he/she showed thanks: ______________________

How it made me feel: ______________________

Who: ______________________

How he/she showed thanks: ______________________

How it made me feel: ______________________

How do you think people feel when you show gratitude towards them? Give an example.

____

____

Name: Date:

Thankfulness

Keep a log of who you want to thank in a day. Then make sure you show your thankfulness to them.

It is worthwhile to make an effort to notice all the things people do for you. Expressing our gratitude to each person may simply mean saying "thanks", phoning, or writing a note.

Thank You Date: ______________

Who I Thank	Why I Thank Him/Her	How I Express My Gratitude (Have I done it or not ✔/✘ ?)

Name: Date:

Trustworthiness

Bounce, Bounce, Rumble, SMASH!

The bouncy bed went down with a crash.

"We can't get caught!" they cried as they fled.

Then Mom arrived and shook her head.

Amanda and her brother told a lie when they said they were not the ones jumping on the bed. When people don't tell the truth or cheat or take something that does not belong to them, they are being untrustworthy.

Of course, their mom knew it was they who bounced on the bed. (Amanda's brother even confessed to taking off his shoes first!) She was disappointed in them for doing something they should not have been doing. But surely their mom would have been happier if they had told the truth.

Name: Date:

Trustworthiness

For each situation, write a sentence explaining what must be done to show trustworthiness.

1. 

2. 

____

____

3. 

____

____

Name: Date:

Trustworthiness

Read what Lily says and answer the questions.

Sometimes people who want to lie about something or steal or cheat on a test pressure us to do the same.

1. Have you ever felt under pressure to lie, cheat, or steal? Give an example.

2. Can you think of a time you gave in to the pressure?

3. If yes, how did you feel afterward?

4. Can you think of a time you resisted the pressure?

5. If yes, how did you feel afterward?

Name: Date:

Trustworthiness

Sometimes we find ourselves in a situation that makes being trustworthy a challenge. Write what you would do in each challenging situation.

1. You know what your brother's birthday present is, and he asks you to tell him. What do you do?

2. Your classmate has the coolest pencils. He has more than he can use, and he left them on his desk beside yours. If you took one, he would never know. What do you do?

3. It's time to do your homework, but your friends are asking you to come out to play. One friend offers to give you his homework for copying. What do you do?

4. There is a cool game at a carnival, but it is for children under eight. The ride attendant invites you to play this game. What do you do?

Name: Date:

Trustworthiness

There are many characteristics that help us to be trustworthy. Complete the trustworthiness pledge by writing the appropriate characteristics on the lines.

honest punctual loyal selfish sincere
self-controlled cooperative self-centred committed dishonest
responsible tolerant patient reliable

Name: Date:

Trustworthiness

Give examples of trustworthiness in your life. Describe what words or actions, by you or others, showed trustworthiness.

Examples of Trustworthiness at Home

Examples of Trustworthiness at School

Examples of Trustworthiness with Friends

Name: Date:

Thoughtfulness

Thoughtfulness is thinking about other people and what they need. Often, thoughtfulness comes naturally, without thinking about it. When other people are hurt, we thoughtfully help them by getting a teacher, or show concern by asking if they are okay. When we respect others, we are being thoughtful.

Sometimes, however, thoughtfulness does not come easily. When we are in a hurry or feeling lazy, it can be hard to think of others. However, we should always try to treat people the way we would like to be treated.

Thoughtfulness is showing concern for ourselves as well as for others. Getting plenty of sleep and eating healthy foods are some of the most thoughtful things we can do for ourselves.

Name: Date:

Thoughtfulness

Draw what is missing in the pictures. Then match the pictures with the correct labels.

- Sharing
- "Get Well" Wishes
- Call to Say "Hello"
- Caring

Name: Date:

Thoughtfulness

Many other characteristics are part of being thoughtful. Cut out the puzzle pieces that contain thoughtful words on the next page. Then glue them to this page.

Thoughtfulness

consideration

sympathy

impatience

laziness

caring

respect

punctuality

kindness

thankfulness

reliability

dishonesty

tolerance

generosity

love

compassion

patience

Name: Date:

Thoughtfulness

Answer these questions.

What are the everyday things you do to be thoughtful?

At Home:

At School:

With My Friends:

Write a sentence to describe the impact your thoughtfulness has had on others.

At Home:

At School:

With My Friends:

Write a sentence to describe the impact others' thoughtfulness has had on you.

Name: Date:

Thoughtfulness

Find a picture of someone performing a thoughtful act from a magazine or newspaper. Cut it out and paste it to the page. Then write a poem about the thoughtfulness in the picture.

A Thoughtful Act

My Poem

Name: Date:

Optimism

Optimism is looking on the bright side, giving more weight to the positive than to the negative. We cannot always control what happens. So, if we want to be happy, we should try to look for the positive in what does happen. It is almost always there.

When we are optimistic, we look forward to the future, and we are certain we can handle whatever it brings.

Name: Date:

Optimism

Write a sentence to describe how each picture shows optimism.

1. 

The cat loses its freedom.

____

____

2. 

George has lots of homework to do.

____

____

3. 

Twenty-five centimetres of snow will fall tomorrow.

____

____

4. 

Tara can't wait to be ten years old.

____

____

Name: Date:

Optimism

Draw a line to connect the optimistic word to its opposite.

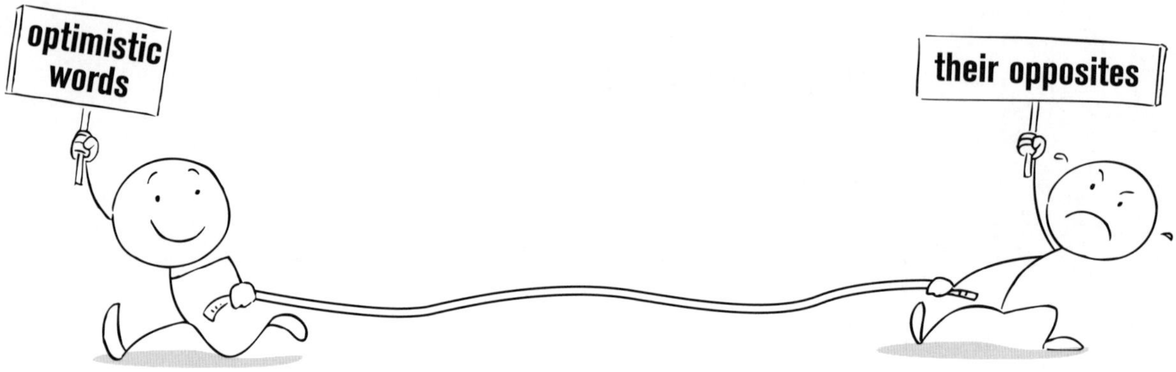

1. optimism •		• doubtful
2. hopeful •		• negative
3. positive •		• upsetting
4. cheerful •		• sad
5. reassuring •		• downbeat
6. upbeat •		• pessimism
7. bright •		• ingratitude
8. encouraging •		• discouraging
9. enthusiasm •		• dark
10. gratitude •		• disinterest

Name: Date:

Optimism

Think about times when you are optimistic. Give two examples of these times. Then answer the question.

Act I I am optimistic about ____________________

____

I show my optimism by ____________________

____

The result of being optimistic ____________________

____

Act II I am optimistic about ____________________

____

I show my optimism by ____________________

____

The result of being optimistic ____________________

____

How is being optimistic a good thing?

____

____

Name: Date:

Optimism

Fill in the blanks with the given words to complete the sentences about optimism. Then cut out the bottom part of this sheet, and stick it to your refrigerator with a magnet.

positive **bright** **hope** **positive** **happy**

Optimism

- Maintain a ________________ attitude.
- Look on the ________________ side of life.
- Have ________________ for the future.
- Have a certain, ________________ manner.
- Look for opportunities to make situations ________________ when they seem to be negative.

Name: Date:

Optimism

Look on the bright side of each situation and write an optimistic sentence to counter each negative one.

1. This homework is going to take me a long time to do.

   ____

2. A new puppy will be a lot of work!

   ____

3. It's too hot to play in the park today.

   ____

4. I won't know anybody at the party.

   ____

5.

Name: Date:

Cooperativeness

Cooperation is working together towards a common goal. Examples of cooperation are sharing, taking turns, and listening to others' ideas.

When we bake cookies with a friend, read aloud to someone, or take turns on the swing, we are showing cooperativeness. We cooperate when we join a soccer team or make room for a sibling on the couch. Agreeing with a neighbour on the type of fence we will share or the foods we will bring to a picnic is cooperation. Our leaders cooperate with other leaders every day to make decisions that affect our lives.

Cooperation makes the world go round!

Name: Date:

Cooperativeness

Observe yourself for a day, and give examples of how you cooperate.

Cut out the sheet below. Fold it two times and keep it with you throughout a day. Keep records of how you showed cooperation.

At Home

___

___

___

___

At School

___

___

___

___

With My Friends / Other Activities

___

___

___

___

Name: Date:

Cooperativeness

Look at the pictures. Write a sentence to explain how the people in the pictures could cooperate. Then explain how cooperation will help.

1.

How could the people cooperate?

___

___

___

How will cooperation help?

___

___

___

2. How could the children cooperate?

___

___

___

George, Jack, and some other children are making a big collage for their class.

How will cooperation help?

___

___

___

Name: Date:

Cooperativeness

There are many benefits to cooperativeness. Think about ways people you know cooperate. Think about how you cooperate.

We cooperate to form a line for our tickets. This helps maintain order and create a peaceful environment.

1. Why is it difficult to cooperate sometimes?

____

____

____

2. In what areas of your life can you cooperate more?

____

____

____

3. How will cooperating more be good for you?

____

____

____

Name: Date:

Cooperativeness

Find examples of cooperativeness from magazines or newspapers. Cut them out and paste them in the box below. You can use words, pictures, or both to share your feelings about cooperation.

Examples of Cooperativeness

My Feelings

Name: Date:

Cooperativeness

Find a partner and cooperate with him/her to give examples of all the items on the list.

My Partner: ____________________

Me: ____________________

- something made by two or more people ____________
- a book written by two or more people ____________
- a team sport ____________
- a chore that requires two or more people ____________
- a job that is done by two or more people ____________
- a song that is sung by two or more singers ____________
- a musical band ____________
- an example of animals cooperating to achieve something ____________
- a school assignment that was completed by two or more people ____________

Name: Date:

Good Manners

I'm learning good manners.
And I don't quite follow.
Do I swallow, then talk?
Or talk, and then swallow?

Should I interrupt
When others are talking?
Is staring good manners?
Or is that gawking?

When my teacher gives homework
Do I ask, "More, please?"
Or is that what I say
When I hear someone sneeze?

As for the homework,
I do know for sure,
What I'd like to say is

"No, thank you, Sir."

Having good manners is not just about being polite. It is behaviour of all kinds that considers the needs and feelings of others.

Name: Date:

Good Manners

What would be a "good manners" response? Write it in the empty speech bubble.

Name: Date:

Good Manners

Find and circle the 18 character traits that lead to good manners.

generosity	determination	empathy	trustworthiness
responsibility	tolerance	flexibility	carelessness
selfishness		fairness	courtesy
reliability	politeness	dishonesty	helpfulness
impoliteness	kindness	greediness	forgiveness
cooperativeness	laziness	respectfulness	boastfulness
thankfulness	patience	grumpiness	honesty

Name: Date:

Good Manners

Read each sentence. Put a checkmark on the line beside the thing you do.

Do you have good manners?

____ I chew with my mouth closed.

____ I don't talk with my mouth full.

____ I use cutlery to eat with.

____ I say "please" and "thank you".

____ I hold doors open for people behind me.

____ I speak politely on the telephone.

____ I don't interrupt when another person is talking.

____ I say "excuse me" when I must interrupt or when someone is blocking my way.

____ I say "may I" instead of "can I" when I am asking for something.

If some of the lines are empty, try to do the things described in those sentences. One day, you will be able to check all the lines.

Name: Date:

Good Manners

Colour the puppets and decorate them. Then cut them out and glue them to popsicle sticks. Practise your good manners with your Good Manners Puppets.

Name: Date:

Good Manners

When we are in a library, we shouldn't talk loudly.

Design a poster that promotes good manners. Decide where you would display the poster. Then think about what words will attract viewers.

Name: Date:

Thriftiness

Thriftiness is making the best use of what you have and making wise choices with what you buy.

Why should we be thrifty? Resources, the things we have and need, are in limited supply. They may cost money, and they may cost the environment through the pollution produced when they are made. They often clutter our rooms and our lives as well, especially when they turn out to be things we don't really need or want. Being thrifty also reduces garbage.

We can be thrifty with our spending by choosing to buy only those things we really need. Many people would have a lot more money to do other things if they did that! Also, taking good care of our belongings means they will not have to be replaced as quickly, or at all. That helps save money and the environment.

Name: Date:

Thriftiness

Check the thrifty choices.

1. There are too many crackers in my lunch.

Ⓐ take some home

Ⓑ feed the birds

Ⓒ throw them away

2. Everyone has purple knee socks!

Ⓐ buy them no matter how much they cost

Ⓑ dye your white knee socks purple

Ⓒ don't do anything; just wear the socks you like

3. The hem of my pants is coming out.

Ⓐ buy new pants

Ⓑ sew the hem

Ⓒ stop wearing pants

4. We're going to the same place.

Ⓐ we'll meet there

Ⓑ we'll see who gets there first

Ⓒ we'll go together

Name: Date:

Thriftiness

Keep a log of your own spending (with your money or your parents' money). Write everything down for a week, including clothes, treats, and gifts.

At the end of the week, highlight everything you didn't really need to buy.

	Items Bought	Money Spent
Sunday		
Monday		
Tuesday		
Wednesday		
Thursday		
Friday		
Saturday		

Name: Date:

Thriftiness

You can use your talents to make your own cards and gifts for friends. Write down your ideas here to plan ahead.

What My Family and Friends Need or Enjoy:

Name	Gift Idea

What I Can...

Make:	*Write:*	*Draw:*

Name: Date:

Thriftiness

Colour the napkin rings. Decide who you are going to give these rings to. Write their names or sentences on the lines to make the napkin rings special.

You may make more napkin rings by tracing the ones below on separate sheets.

Name: Date:

Thriftiness

Check your level of thriftiness by checking off your thrifty ways. Then colour the boxes to match the number of checkmarks that you have put on the lines.

Am I Thrifty?

____ I take good care of my clothes, old and new.

____ I give away clothes that no longer fit.

____ I accept hand-me-down clothes in good shape from others.

____ I put away my toys and books so that they stay in good shape.

____ I keep my room tidy so my belongings aren't misplaced.

____ I look for things I need at second-hand stores first.

____ I borrow books from the library instead of buying them new.

____ I don't ask for things I don't need.

____ I make my own cards and gifts for family and friends.

____ I am careful to not be so thrifty that I am stingy.

Level of Thriftiness

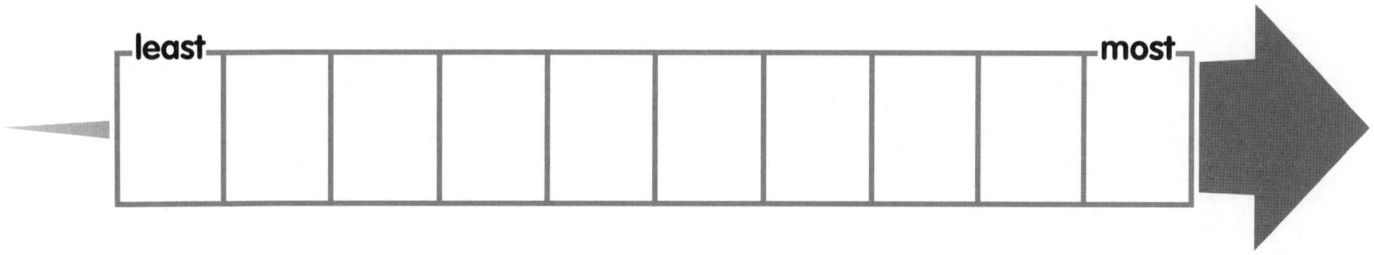

Canadian Character Education
Grades 3-4

Project Ideas

My Teammates

Think about an activity that you participated in as a team player. It might have been a choir, a basketball team, or a science project. Find a picture of you with your teammates and glue it onto a poster board. Then introduce your teammates and yourself to others. Tell everyone how you and your teammates coorperated to reach a goal and worked as a team.

We know cooperation is in effect when we hear the words "team" or "partner". Many sports and businesses need teamwork and partnership to function properly. These aspects make it fun to work and play with others.

The Power of "Thank You"

Make a book recording situations where you said "thank you" and the names of the people you thanked. Do it for a month.

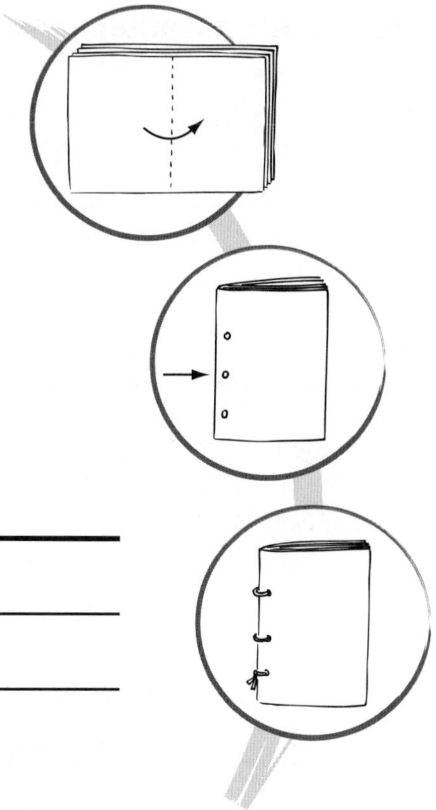

Steps to Making Your Book:

1. Get four pieces of paper and fold them in half.
2. Punch three holes along the folded lines.
3. Tie the paper together with strings.
4. Draw a table as below on each page.

Date	I thanked...	Situation

After a month, check the book to see how many times you said "thank you". When you treated people politely, did they seem friendlier towards you?

Knowing More about Myself – Page 1

Write your name on the cards below and on the next page. Cut them out and give one card to a person who knows you well. Ask him or her to circle the character traits that you show. Then collect all your cards.

What characters traits do you have and what character traits should you work on?

______________ 's Character Traits

Kindness **Patience** **Tolerance** **Thankfulness**
Politeness **Courtesy** **Courage** **Determination**
Cheerfulness **Helpfulness** **Responsibility**
Optimism **Perseverance** **Thriftiness**

______________ 's Character Traits

Kindness **Patience** **Tolerance** **Thankfulness**
Politeness **Courtesy** **Courage** **Determination**
Cheerfulness **Helpfulness** **Responsibility**
Optimism **Perseverance** **Thriftiness**

Knowing More about Myself – Page 2

_______________ 's Character Traits

Kindness Patience Tolerance Thankfulness
Politeness Courtesy Courage Determination
Cheerfulness Helpfulness Responsibility
Optimism Perseverance Thriftiness

_______________ 's Character Traits

Kindness Patience Tolerance Thankfulness
Politeness Courtesy Courage Determination
Cheerfulness Helpfulness Responsibility
Optimism Perseverance Thriftiness

_______________ 's Character Traits

Kindness Patience Tolerance Thankfulness
Politeness Courtesy Courage Determination
Cheerfulness Helpfulness Responsibility
Optimism Perseverance Thriftiness

_______________ 's Character Traits

Kindness Patience Tolerance Thankfulness
Politeness Courtesy Courage Determination
Cheerfulness Helpfulness Responsibility
Optimism Perseverance Thriftiness

Representing Animals

Do this project with a partner. Give three positive character traits you think your partner possesses. Think of a different animal to represent each character trait. Give reasons why you chose the animals to represent the corresponding character traits. Then find pictures of the animals from old magazines and newspapers and cut them out. Organize the pictures and glue them onto some construction paper.

Punch three holes along the edge of the construction paper and tie them up with a ribbon. Then give it to your partner.

Materials
- construction paper
- old magazines or newspapers
- markers and crayons
- scissors and glue
- pencil and ruler
- strings (ribbons)

You may add captions to the pictures to let your partner know what character traits he or she and the animals have in common.

Doing My Best

Think about what areas of your life you would like to work on. Choose one and copy the table below on a piece of cardboard. Find a partner to work with to help you reach your goals. Have your partner sign your board when he or she has witnessed your achievement.

Doing My Best

I would like to do better at ________________________.

My goal is to ________________________.

3 steps I need to take in order to reach my goal are:

1. ________________________
2. ________________________
3. ________________________

My Action Plan:	Completion Date	Sign
Step 1: ________________ ________________	________	________
Step 2: ________________ ________________	________	________
Step 3: ________________ ________________	________	________

****You may draw pictures on the cardboard to illustrate your effort, too.***

My Character Traits – Page 1

Think of a person in your class who has the character trait mentioned on each slip of paper. Write that person's name on it. Each person's name can only be written once. Then cut out the paper slips and give them to the corresponding classmates.

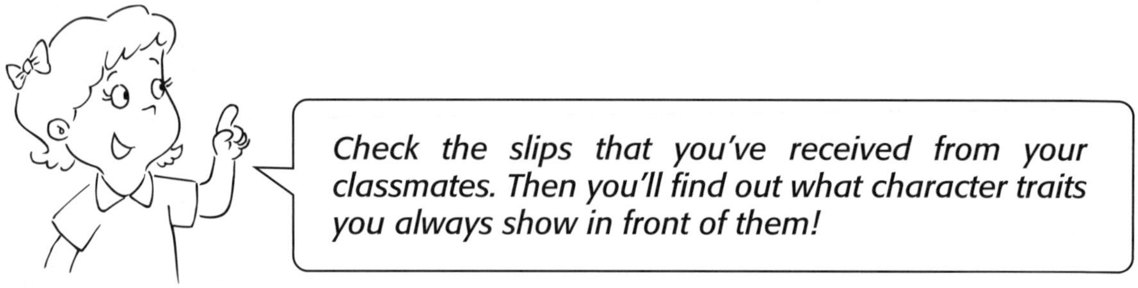

Kind	Forgiving	Intelligent	Responsible
Creative	Patient	Cheerful	Friendly

My Character Traits – Page 2

Honest	Helpful	Gentle
Hardworking	Polite	Respectful
Trustworthy	Generous	Cooperative
Compassionate	Courageous	Thoughtful